POWER BREEDS ABUSE
i.e. Power Leads To Corruption

Table Of Contents

Introduction 3
Evolutionary History 4
Pride and Prejudice 6
Assault on Freedom 7
American Monarchy 9
EPA & Spilled Milk 11
Unconstitutional Actions 12
Hiding behind Privilege 14
Getting a Perspective 16
Infamous Quotes 17
Feedback from Iraq 18
The Scott McClellan Affair 19
More Bush Brilliance 21
Pluses and Minuses 23
Supreme Principles 25
Follow the Leader 29
Business Rip Offs 30
Knowledge Suppression 31
The Balance of Power 34
Insider Trading 36
The Eric Holder Affair 37
Corporate Coziness 38
Rampant Leniency 41
Kip's Books & Links 42

Introduction

Power is the ability/facility to do something. With machines, that can mean getting work done. With humans it means taking advantage of others who have fewer resources at their disposal, in big and little ways. In big business it means foregoing ethics in a chase after the dollar and ever higher profits. In politics it means doing whatever it takes to get reelected, by virtually everyone who is engaged in that profession. In the upper echelons of government it means bending or breaking the rules, and then hoping not to get caught at that activity. One of the ways that this comes about is when rules and laws are soft-pedaled or ignored by the regulators in order to ingratiate ones self to those who are supposed to be made to conform.

While most of us live in socially acceptable environments, and get along there quite well. There are a few of us who will not hesitate to disadvantage others for their own personal gain or gratification. Some of these people, who are involved in Ponzi type schemes and insider trading scams, have justified their lack of concern for the lost revenue that is suffered by their victims. These people are so captivated with their own personal wealth that they have become desensitized to the hardships which they dole out to others. Even the very real possibility of doing jail time is not always a sufficient deterrent.

Because the siren song of power is so pervasive, such as with the ills that are widespread in politics, we tend to cast a blind eye toward the victims, seeing this as just part of life. That would be until it happens to you or someone close to you.

The following text details just a few of the issues and causes that beset American institutions in their quest for power and advantage.

Evolutionary History

There appears to be a gene or two that are responsible for our having self-centered behaviors. No doubt they aided in our early survival because selfishness was not always a bad thing. Similarly, a set of genes appears to have developed into an instinct that allows us to generate the hierarchy-of-concern that we manifest toward others. This behavior, which is taken as natural, is that...
-- we care for ourselves first and foremost | though this can be temporarily set aside when we try to save the life of another, for example
-- we care somewhat less for those who are the closest to us
-- and so on down the line until we get to the many, who we may not seriously care about at all

While this attitude seems to be obvious and normal, it is not quite that simple. Evolution played a staring role in its development based on trial and error. In our early history we had successes and failures relating to who were the most essential friends for survival and who were not. This knowledge eventually led to developing the mentioned hierarchical attitude. This trait is acceptable today, not because it involves any sort of universal truth… it is just the evolution of pragmatism.

Theodosious Dobzhanshy, geneticist: *"Nothing in biology makes sense, except in the light of evolution."*

The curious part about defining who friends are is that it can be highly anti-social. If we are given the choice of saving the life of a loved one or saving the lives of a dozen strangers, it may be the twelve that would bite the dust. This is the emotional-logic side of decision making, as opposed to the rational-logic aspect of our brain. Because we do not have the same connection with people that are not familiar to us, we do not have as strong an empathy for them or an overriding commitment to their survival. Rationally speaking, twelve lives are worth more than one, but we have not evolved to make that kind of judgment.

An example of rational-logic thinking *(for which no judgment is offered)* was expressed years ago by a social scientist. He

4

suggested that feeding the starving people in Africa was counter-productive to their survival in areas with abject poverty. It was his conclusion that for every one who was kept from hunger and death, ten more will be born that might in turn starve to death. He believed that some Africans are on a counter-productive path, perhaps for a variety of reasons, in which more of them will starve each year. And if this lesson applies to Africa today, perhaps it is only a matter of time before it applies to the rest of us as we outpace our resources.

While our emotional-logic thinking may have served us well during our tribal days, such as with the concept of protect your peers but not the strangers, it is not nearly as valuable a tool in today's world. Our social network has become so interconnected that we can no longer afford to have this perspective about who is and who is not a friend. Imagine what civilization would be like if we were not to care for others during natural disasters just because we do not know the victims. Very quickly people and countries could become pitted against one another in destructive ways.

An example of this kind of negative behavior can still be found with tribes of the Arabian Deserts that do not cultivate even rudimentary concern for their neighbors, instead preferring to exhibit aggressive behaviors *(perhaps due to sparse resources and indoctrinatio*n) toward each other. Their lack of empathy has led to generations of religious confrontations and ethnic cleansing. They will occasionally kill the *others* because they can not tolerate competing religions *(even though they are similar)* in their midst.

Pride and Prejudice

Years ago George Bush made what appeared to be a close friendship with Russia's Tsar-mentality President Putin. I guess his *pride* was telling him that he might be able to achieve what Regan had accomplished some years earlier, which was nudging Russia into becoming a more democratic state.

As events have turned out, Putin has been responsible for major backpedaling of democracy rather than on liberalizing it. Adverse political news in Russia is routinely suppressed, and dissidents are harassed and jailed. Apparently this lesson of runaway power is lost on some of us. Both of the Bush administrations presided over the gradual erosion of personal freedoms that make America what it is… free.

Just because politicians have been elected to office does not imply that they are knowledgeable, clever, don't have *prejudices*, or are even quick studies of difficult situations. This additionally holds true for the government agencies that are run by ex-politicians and political appointees. Just look to the reports of the blunders that were made by CIA and FBI over the years as proof of this thesis, such as with Iraq having weapons of mass destruction.

Because we reside in a so-called representative democracy, most people remain detached from government workings, and they simply choose to imagine that all is being managed well, without having a need for citizen intervention. Could we be more wrong?

Assault on Freedom

Thanks to the some provisions of the Patriot Act we have seen multiple assaults on our telephone conversations and emails without Court warrants… laws that have been deemed to be unconstitutional by many. As a case in point, we have permitted the communication companies to bug American's phones, and then they have been given immunity from prosecution for those efforts. And if these assaults are indeed unconstitutional, who is working on our side to stop that transgression?

GWB used another provision of this act, via his Attorney General *(AG)* Gonzales, to stack US Attorney's offices with his like-minded lawyers without the traditionally required advice and consent of Congress. A number of standing attorneys were unceremoniously and unjustifiably sacked to make way for those conservatives who would more closely follow a political line, as opposed to a legal line.

The emails that definitively demonstrated a conscious plan to dump the attorneys *(contrary to the AG's statements to the press and his sworn statements to Congress)* were "accidentally" deleted from Justice Department *(JD)* computers. Backup retention of these emails is required by law for the public record, but that did not stop the chief law enforcement officer of the US from being associated with criminal deletions.

As is a familiar scenario with government, no one has been prosecuted for that loss of that data. In 2010 an announcement by the Justice Department stated that the AG *(their boss)* would not be prosecuted for his participation in the firing and replacement of attorneys… another example of politicians taking care of their peer group. Just another *eighteen minutes of missing tape* for those who remember the White House secretary's alleged lapse during Watergate.

A side story is the role of Monica Gooding, an aid to Gonzales. A US Attorney in Washington complained that she had tried to block the hiring of an attorney because of her prejudice against a person that was perceived to be a liberal Democrat. When incriminating emails surfaced and her complicity in the matter could no longer be denied, she broke down into tears saying "All I ever wanted to do was serve this President".   So her version of serving America is to pervert the **justice** system into a **just-us** system for the benefit of a President.

If the aids to Bush were so willing to circumvent the law, where does this dishonorable behavior come from? The clear answer is that behavioral examples flow down from the top.

We should recognize how important it is that the JD be fair and impartial without succumbing to political influence… that is all of us except for Bush and company, apparently. While the JD lawyers can be fired at will, the longstanding policy has been that they have their jobs for life. This unwritten agreement goes a long way toward guaranteeing their impartiality and resistance to political persuasion. People from the JD have testified that its mission had been seriously perverted by hiring politically oriented lawyers and firing existing, career lawyers.

Rev. Martin Luther King Jr., social activist: *"Injustice anywhere is a threat to justice everywhere."*

American Monarchy

While presidential excesses are by no means limited to Obama, he has set a benchmark for over the top travel spending at the taxpayers expense. It is not just foreign royalties that fly with a fleet of luxurious jets to far off destinations for a few hours rather than using the phone to conduct their business. Are you aware that his frequent travels include…

-- the best trained Air Force pilots and their staffs/ground-crews

-- a second jumbo jet for the press *(so that they keep their mouth's shut?)* and other VIPs?

-- several planes for the president's many vehicles and staffers

-- airplanes to bring in gasoline tanker trucks for the president's planes to guarantee that the fuel is not tampered with

-- contingents of anti-terrorist military located along motorcade routes

-- copious supplies - ranging from lighting, to red carpets, which are just the tip of equipment-iceberg

-- Michelle Obama taking her hairdresser *(can she no longer comb her own hair?)*, along with a large contingent of superfluous staffers

-- vacation trips to Hawaii that have been reported to cost taxpayers about $1.5 million per trip

-- a trip was made to Africa in order to underscore the president's commitment to malaria containment *(I guess the phones were down that day)*

-- in the first weeks of the nuclear problem in Japan, Obama played golf and took his family on a trip to Brazil. Does that remind anyone of the Bush's lack of reaction to Katrina?

In the election year of 2012 Obama used the travel resources of the White House to make various trips to swing states at the taxpayer's expense. The House Speaker, Boehner, criticized these trips as merely political, which if true they must by federal law be paid for by Obama's election campaign. One of the trips was said to be nothing more than a fake fight with congress regarding federally funded student loan rates.

The president has the resources of regular press events at which he could easily voice his concerns, either directly or through the White House press office. So we end up paying millions of dollars for his lavish trips which are purely political in nature, and then the president lies *(implicitly and explicitly)* about their need for the public benefit… obviously without remorse over their costs. This *entitled* person can never spend too much to become embarrassed, apparently.

The above reminds me of the television program American Greed where the felons show no concern for the people that they fleece. When politicians are given an unlimited piggy bank they seem to have no compunction about spending as much as they choose.

EPA & Spilled Milk

Under the: *it doesn't get sillier* category, the Environment Protection Agency *(EPA)* has determined that since milk contains oil *(butterfat)* it falls under their purview of their regulation. Then to top that wisdom off, they ruled that the EPA has the authority to force farmers to comply with its rules to file "emergency regulations plans" in order to illustrate how they will cope with spilled milk. This includes showing the methods they will use to train first responders and to build containment facilities. Can our regulators get any more outrageous then this? Are the nut jobs in control, or what?

Unconstitutional Actions

Another political threat to our freedoms involves an action that was ostensibly motivated by the threat of terrorism. It regards Bush's issuance of Executive Orders *(EOs)*, which are commands that carry the force of law behind them. Wait a minute. Isn't that supposed to be Congress's job? One of these overreaching EOs signed by Bush stated that all US regulatory commissions must have a Policy Advisor *(PA)* supplied by the White House. Does that remind anyone of Russia's need to have political officers checking on its generals and bureaucrats?

Apparently these PA's will be in place to make their own laws by reinterpreting existing laws. This might not be so dire if it weren't for the fact that these people were spineless *yes* people employed to further Bush's political and religious agendas. This packing method is not much different from the Court stacking that has been done by Caesar Chavez of Venezuela, or that was attempted by Franklin Roosevelt when he tried to grab power to promote his New Deal agenda. You may recall that he wanted to nominate one additional Supreme Court Justice for each sitting judge over seventy years old. This would have amounted to a dilution of the votes of those judges who had opposed his plans.

Most Americans probably feel that they had nothing much to fear from Bush's frame of mind, and wanted their government to take more effective actions against world terrorism. This sounds good on paper, but freedom is not a guarantee. There will always be some who are willing to take pieces of it away from us.

I can just imagine hearing the weasel-brained advisors whispering into Bush's ear telling him how easy it would be to circumvent Congressional authority with EOs. They might even have pointed out that because the legislature is typically slow to react and is not up to speed on what's happening inside the Oval Office, EOs would be an expedient way to promote an agenda without concern for Congress overriding a veto. The Nixon administration demonstrated a similar disregard for legalities when they authorized the Watergate break-in.

In 2014 Obama announced that he would use EOs to unilaterally grant amnesty to millions of illegal immigrants that are already in this country. The reaction of congress was fast and furious, and as usual for this body, mere bluster. However, in response to this presidential overreach of authority, the Sheriff of Maricopa County Arizona, Joe Arpaio, has sued the feds on the justification that these orders are unconstitutional. That is why we have a congress.

The lesson here for us may be that it is up to the public to act in government matters because our congresspersons have once again proved themselves to be incapable of providing the services to their country that they were hired to do. We need a public service organization, paid for with donations from concerned citizens and groups, which will take the necessary legal steps to insure that the government does not overstep it mandate.

Hiding behind Privilege

The Supreme Court, in its wisdom, has ruled that the Office of the President has legitimate reasons to keep some conversations from becoming public. The purported logic is that Presidential confidants and foreign agents need the freedom to speak their minds without the threat that they will exposed to the world. So far so good if one buys into that self-serving argument about government secrecy and then ignores its very real impact. Political decisions should not be kept from the public except when forming a strategy against an aggressor or perhaps with some personnel issues. However, we have lived with the unnecessary principle of government secrecy for so long that it is unlikely to be supplanted any time soon.

There have been a number of Presidents who found it expedient to take advantage of the Courts ruling on secrecy in order to hide their dubious behaviors behind this privilege. Bush used this subterfuge to cover up the events surrounding the firing of a number of US Attorneys and his justification for going to war with Iraq. He also ordered people in his administration to disregard subpoenas authorized by Congress in their search for malfeasance at the Justice Department. There was no actual national security risk at stake in this last case, just the prevention of an open government where unlawful behaviors could be exposed.

GWB also ordered people in his administration to disregard those subpoenas authorized by congress in their search for malfeasance at the Justice Department. There was no actual national security risk at stake in this case, just the prevention of an open government where unlawful behaviors could be exposed. Secrecy is rarely appropriate in any setting, and it is even less so in government. It is dangerous to the public at times.

One populist backlash to the mentality and vastness of state secrets has been the establishment of the website Wikileaks. Its stated goal is to remove the veil of secrecy from government and force it to operate in the clear light of day. But the bureaucrats are busy doing what they can to stop that free flow of information which includes going after the site's creator, removing the website from the Internet, and prosecuting contributors to it.

15

Getting a Perspective

Bin-Ladin and company may have killed thousand of people in the World Trade Center, but the war in Iraq and Afghanistan had killed even more Americans… over 6000 through 2011. Sadam Hussein may have murdered tens of thousands in an effort to tame his real or imagined detractors and maintain control of the country's contentious religious factions, but his absence from power has resulted in the deaths of tens of thousands more. This information is not to justify these actions but to put them into perspective…
-- Have any of the deaths in Iraq been worth the price?
-- Has the Bush/Obama war accomplished much beyond the increased aggression by many of the world's Muslims?
-- Has it made the world a safer place in which to live?

Isn't it interesting that Bush, who professed his adherence to God's law and to pro-life should be the same person that presided over a killing war that has lasted longer than WWII. Rather than conducting ourselves as one nation among equals, he preferred to act out his military fantasies at our countries' expense. One by one the Western countries making up the original allied coalition became disenchanted as they came to realize the futility and counter-productivity of the war. It's to bad that they played follow the leader for as long as they did.

Infamous Quotes

Regarding the conflict in Iraq, Laura Bush had the arrogance to say on more than one occasion that "No one suffers more than George and I do over the war". This outrageous statement was even more disingenuous while they lived in their isolated, pampered, monarchy-like accommodations. I guess the deep sorrow of the relatives and friends of these dead soldiers didn't count for much in their minds. Is it that these two lightweight thinkers were completely out of touch? Or is it that they were unable to understand the difference between telling the truth and telling a lie?

Adlai E Stevenson, politician: *"Those who corrupt the public mind are just as evil as those who steal from the public purse."*

A comment that had been made many times by GWB while referring to the terrorists has been: "They hate us for our freedom". Pardon me? Is there anything even remotely logical or sincere about that statement? Maybe they also hate us for playing tennis, not eating our pets, and using toilet paper. Surely it couldn't be that they hate us for invading their land and supporting their enemy Israel. Perhaps he also believed that they crave making war and we were a convenient target. He also showed a considerable lack of insight when he called the terrorists "cowards", ignoring that they…
-- have a deep religious faith
-- will not permit foreigners on their soil
-- will carefully plan an offence
-- will give up their life for a cause
Those sure are some cowards.

Those sure are some cowards. Statements like those which GWB made boil down to a transparent attempt to deflect us from the truth about our aggressive military-industrial-complex and our appetite for foreign oil. Those are the real bad guys.

True believers are among the most dangerous people on the planet because they will not listen to reason, much less understand it.

Feedback from Iraq

A few years ago I communicated with a person from Iraq while I was playing online bridge. I asked him how he felt about what the Americans were doing in his country. Without any hesitation his reply was that: "Sadam's hell was far better than Bush's paradise". This concept of living with the lesser of evils is apparently lost on the illogical minds of our leaders.

The Scott McClellan Affair

Talk about shooting the messenger… Before the ink was dry on his tell-all book "What Happened", the spin doctors in the Bush administration *(which I suppose was basically all of them)* were busy casting aspersions back in the direction of McClellan. Their testy comments did not deny the facts of the book as much as they painted Scott as a person who…
-- was only interested in the money
-- hadn't complained to Bush's staff in the past about problems
-- showed a lack of loyalty to the President *(since when is loyalty more important than truth?)*
-- waited too long before coming forward

When the book was published, Scott revealed that the Bush Administration had regularly fed talking points to sympathetic members of the press *(probably no surprise here),* and that the press did not reveal the sources of those stories. What this amounted to is the dissemination of propaganda by an administration in concert with the press in order to color the news in a way that was favorable to them. This would not be as disgraceful had it been accompanied by disclosure of where the news had come from. However that was not the case.

Going back to the assaults on McClellan's integrity, let's say that it was all about the money. So What! Can anyone point out a politician who is not in it for the money, unless they are already wealthy? And then they are in it for the raw power of the office. It is nothing less than hypocrisy for people to throw stones at others regarding a topic that they are guilty of themselves.

Other criticisms leveled against McClellan were similarly weak and did nothing to enlighten the public. What these disingenuous arguments by Bush's staff were designed to do was to obfuscate the issues that McClellan had raised by creating a smokescreen of counter-charges. Then the press obliged these bullies in their cover-up by endlessly repeating the trumped up rebuttals, regardless of the fact that they were irrelevant and half truths. It is only important what Bush did or didn't do… not what McClellan did or didn't do. But the press never got that concept, presumably not wanting to offend the administration that they rely on for their bread and butter.

One of the interesting aspects of the "What Happened" book is the allegation that V.P. Cheney ordered McClellan to exonerate Libby for his role in the Valerie Plame affair *(the outed CIA agent whose husband had criticized the administration)*. How many more behind-the-scenes adventures Cheney was a participant in may never be known? What stands out is the arrogance that he displays whenever he is questioned about his part in various controversies.

One might think that Cheney's friends and associates would keep him at a distance after witnessing his lack of integrity in action. Since that appears not to be the case, we might properly assume that there is a society of business and government leaders who believe that they can act as they see fit, and that our normal rules of conduct and laws do not apply to them.

More Bush Brilliance

Among other thoughtless stuff, GWB apparently saw an opportunity to democratize the Middle East, and he showed little interest in what the repercussions of that mindset could be, such as…
-- raising the nation debt to astounding levels
-- being responsible for the deaths of tens of thousands
-- arming the terrorists with a cause to fight for
-- inflating the price of energy

In fact GWB did not even understand that the Muslims are not nearly as interested in democracy as they are in their belief in the Qu'ran. So much for his research staff.

Presidents Johnson and Bush were faced with the same quandary regarding ending wars that they inherited or initiated. How could we cut and run, then dishonor those who had already died, was the lament. Did they imagine that the next soldier who might die would reflect on those who have already died in vain if he could save his own life? And even if he were so illogical as to think that his sacrifice was reasonable, would that be justification for even one more unnecessary death?

History can be a weak validation for current behavior when it comes to war. The only question that matters is: *does continued fighting help or hurt this country*? No other argument need be taken into account. This question is analogous to the decision that should be made when deciding whether or not to sell a stock… Is the sale correct today? A rational thought process should be taken without any regard to the original purchase price or to those who have died. History is irrelevant in these cases.

How did we get ourselves into Iraq in the first place? The most likely answer is oil. Iraq has plenty of it and we wanted protected and available, perhaps at a dirt cheap price. We didn't go there to…
-- rescue the people from a harsh dictator - they can be found throughout the world
-- prevent the proliferation of weapons of mass destruction - there were none

-- bring democracy to a people who craved it - they are actually suspicious of democracy

The end result of our intervention was that the price of oil, which hovered around $30 per barrel, went incredibly higher, and not just for the US but for all of the oil purchasing nations. Don't you think they love us for that? And how do you think those extra dollars per barrel are being used? Possibly against us by the Arab nations that would like to see us taken down a peg?

An even more serious result of our starting this conflict was the awakening and emboldening of a religious subculture *(much like the Japanese awakened America, the sleeping giant, in WWII)* whose goal is to dominate the Middle East. There are factions that want to spread their "true" religion by any means possible. And because of our actions, we have provided them with the motivation and recruiting environment that they could scarcely dream of providing on their own.

In 2009 the Secretary of the Navy said at a ship commissioning "No matter how many times you attack us, we will always come back." Do we really need to come back? Do we need to be the policemen of the world? Since there are some who understand the implications of this detrimental scenario that we have created for ourselves, isn't it curious that this logic not hit Washington in any big way? And why not? Just who is responsible for continuing this farce? The hundreds of billion dollars we spend go somewhere. Perhaps we should follow the money.

Pluses and Minuses

For a good many years this country had led the world in nearly every category that is important to us... scientific research, education, healthcare, retirement, automobiles, manufacturing, nuclear power, gas and oil production, electronics, etc. Today we are so far down the line on many of these lists that we are beginning to look like a second world county.

About all we are really good at is building some better war toys for the military-industrial-complex, as well as selling ourselves those goods that we buy from other countries. These activities do not generate the consumer products that can directly contribute to our economic welfare. They only encouraged the likes of the Johnsons, Bushes and Obamas in their foreign misadventures, quests for oil, and tolerating those multi-national companies that outsource work to foreign countries.

Then we use our toys to intimidate countries, and spend vastly more to insure the security that we have voluntarily put into jeopardy. How obscene it that?

I hold congress immensely accountable for our problems with their decades of...
-- insufficient spending on the replacement of our deteriorating infrastructure
-- excessive spending on political pork and worthless projects
-- legislation that serves the privileged
-- setting their party lines above the needs of the country

So one has to ask...
-- Are there any fewer illegal drugs available because of the billions that have been spent by the dupes at the DEA?
-- Doesn't it cost billions to house the criminals that we have created with our drug policies?
-- Have our much needed healthcare costs ever gone down?
-- Has the highway infrastructure or its congestion improved?
-- Are there fewer immigrants crossing over from Mexico?
-- Have we made significant inroads into renewable resources?
...need I go on?

This irrationality has helped take us to the point where our country is trillions of dollars in debt *vs.* $800 billion when Regan took office. And this debt has an astounding interest bill that can not easily be paid down for decades or centuries to come.

Because politicians have treated themselves and their wealthy friends so well for so long, we can't guarantee that the Social Security program will be intact when the current crop of boomers wants to retire *(at the current rate of about 1000 per day)*. Because we are living on credit, our huge tax burden will ultimately be passed along to our children and to their children's children. How would you like it if your parents left *you* deeply in debt?

Supreme Principles

We would like to believe that the Supreme Court is composed of nine intelligent, impartial jurists who will be willing and equipped to cast decisions that are equitable, reasonable and in accordance with our Constitution. But if this were even half true, why would all Presidents be so anxious to make these appointments? The answer is that members of the Court come with their own biases, and they will be selected for their having attitudes that conform to the nominating President, regardless of any faithfulness to Constitutional obligations. Their integrity is often overshadowed by their agenda.

While it is impossible for anyone to be completely unbiased, some of us have a greater problem with this discipline than others. Judges and lawyers are typically appointed or elected for their beliefs rather than for their impartially. Presidents are known for trying to stack the Court in their philosophical favor. When like-minded candidates are installed, reinterpretation of the constitution is possible.

Fair and balanced… a fanciful flower that rarely blossoms

An example of agenda-peddling by the Supreme Court in favor of big business came up regarding the whistleblower legislation. In its wisdom the Court ruled 6 to 2 that a particular tattler was not entitled to recover money for his fraud exposure because he lacked "direct and independent knowledge upon which his allegations were based". Sounds like double-talk that was designed to circumvent an important law enacted by Congress, and which serves a pressing need.

The law was passed to penalize those companies that are involved in illegal behavior, and to encourage those who will come forward with incriminating evidence. Do we really care how they came by their information, short of breaking and entering? The method of their discovery is hardly the point. But the Supreme Court saw fit to limit the whistleblower legislation based on a business-friendly, illogical, anti-consumer posture. Tattlers will now have less incentive to offer their service *(risking termination for no profit),* and the offending companies will be more immune from prosecution.

In another decision the Court's 5 to 4 ruling overturned a long-standing ban on companies being able to set minimum prices for the vendors of their products. This price fixing scheme had previously been legislated to be illegally anti-competitive because companies could raise the price floor for their products in concert with other vendors or distributors. In the Court's ruling, price floor setting could be either competitive *(really?)* or non-competitive. So in their minds, a turn-about from the previous law was not necessarily anti-trust in nature. Apparently the Supreme Court would have us believe that price fixing schemes can occasionally be beneficial to the consumer, but don't count on it.

This Court decision can be seen as support for reduced business competition because of a counterfeit rationale. So the Court showed how easily it ends up in the pocket of big business and antagonistic to consumers. Do you see this as part of the good ol' boys club?

Curiously, a pricing practice has gone unchallenged for some time in the garment industry and probably elsewhere. Not only do major suppliers to large department stores dictate the décor of the selling areas that are dedicated to their products, but they may also tell those retailers what the selling prices will be, and how much and when the items can be marked down. Anti-trust? What else?

Recently I used the Internet to find the best price on a hepa *(air purifier)* filter and discovered that every seller of a particular brand had exactly the same price… that is every seller in the US. This universal price setting is not prima-facie anti-competitive if you believe the Court.

Then in 2010 a Supreme Court decision "Citizens United v. Federal Election Commission" it struck down a provision of the McCain-Feingold election law. That law had prohibited corporations and unions from purchasing broadcast time for election matter that named a candidate within 30 days of a primary and 60 days of a general election. This decision freed up corporations and unions to spend unlimited amounts on "electioneering communications". In addition, the donors were not required to be identified. The rationale behind this change was that most of this political spending occurs outside of contributions to a candidate's campaign, and that the campaigns were not accountable for the veracity, or lack of such, with the "communications". Really?

What the Court did require is that there must be a "wall" between these Super PACs and the campaigns they favor. This is, of course, a flight of fantasy since their activity can not be controlled when it is done surreptitiously. And there is no government firewall in place that would prevent those communications. In 2012 John McCain said "I predict to you that there will be huge scandals associated with this huge flood of money".

The justification by the Supreme Court was that their decision was based on freedom of speech principles. Did they ever think of balancing probable corruption against the interests of the people? The classic analogy in opposition to this ruling is the prohibition against yelling *fire* in a theatre. And then there is the undeniable consideration that this money will be flowing from the super rich in concert with their interests, which are unlikely to be those of the rest of us. Could the Court be any more wrong-headed?

To its credit, the Court did rebuke the Bush administration for years of stonewalling on acknowledging global warming. The EPA had presented the Court with a list of ludicrous reasons why they declined to take action on automobile and truck emissions. One of the more specious arguments was that auto pollution is not deemed to be poisonous. That's news to me. How about you? Maybe these deep thinkers were standing behind someone's tailpipe for too long.

More likely is it that the EPA bureaucrats owed their allegiance to the administration instead of to the public. Then in its wisdom the EPA suggested that this matter should be resolved using a voluntary approach *(haven't we heard that nonsense before?)*, rather than by regulation. I believe we know how proactive and inclined to making changes for the better the auto industry has been throughout the years. Not! The Court ruling was just 5 to 4 in favor of a critical environmental issue... one that should have been a 9-zip slam-dunk. This split should make us wonder what the agenda of the opposition judges was. Perhaps the Court's philosophy is about not restraining big businesses on whatever they deem to be in their interest, as apposed to what is in the best interest of consumers.

28

Follow the Leader

What the previously mentioned abuses of power demonstrate is the ubiquitous dearth of ethics and integrity that pervades our society. This can happen for any number reasons. Because it takes a degree of cunning to achieve high position *(whether in a corporate or government environment)*, the effort instills a pattern of slick behavior that may stay with those who succumb to the addiction of power.

Once some level achievement has been obtained, an executive can look around and see how often others have manipulated the system to get where they are. The message for many is clear. If others can do it with little or no retribution, why then why oh why can't I. Many of us may look at the leaders of business and government for examples on how to conduct ourselves in public and private. If we have not been privy to enlightened mentoring or strong principles in childhood, the perceived benefits of corruption can be influential on our adult formation. This can be the outcome when we take note that...
-- all presidents lie to the public with impunity
-- great numbers of our political and business leaders become embroiled in corruption
-- far too many institutions are pleasuring their top officers with hundred of millions of dollars in salaries and bonuses

So whether society admits it or not, corruption trickles down from the top and pollutes those below. And we do so little to stem the tide.

Business Rip Offs

In 2010 it was reported that several insurance companies had taken advantage of the relatives of deceased soldiers. They managed the death benefits, earned some 5% on these accounts, and then paid out about 1% in interest to the relatives. The retained difference amounted to nice windfall for this handful of companies. A class action suit was eventually initiated to recover these ill-gotten gains. This is only one example out of many on how big business can be corrupted by its quest for ever greater profits.

The home/small-office printer and ink cartridge business is an excellent case of an all-too-clever business plan with their: *set prices low now - get large profits in the future scheme* - one that we should all be aware of. There are many other companies that function in this devious way. Basically the game is to price the non-disposable part of a product near or below the cost of manufacture to encourage sales, then make up for the tiny profit or initial loss with the highly profitable, disposable items that are used by these products.

Printers and ink cartridges are a part of this notorious business plan. In a few cases these printers are priced below the cost of their replacement printer cartridges. In one particular case a new printer was priced at about 30 percent less than the cost of its cartridges. For my printers I have chosen to purchase cartridges from a third party supplier at a significant discount. The potential downside to this method can be the loss of warranty *(who cares)* and products that some *(mostly printer manufacturers)* allege may shorten a printer's lifespan. I have experienced a few faulty cartridges that were replaced, but have not yet had a printer problem.

Knowledge Suppression

Information the public should know about is occasionally suppressed by the news media, politicians, corporations, and government agencies because it is in their interest to do so. This distortion occurs because…
-- the news media is beholding to politicians and agencies who feed them propaganda
-- government agencies are obligated to politicians who fund their money-wasting bureaucracies
-- politicians are indebted to the large corporations who pull the strings with their campaign financing *(bribes)*
-- large corporations are obliged to, well to no one actually, because they are truly the owners of government

These circumstances add up to the incestuous relationships that conspire to suppress meaningful information from being disclosed to the public and keeping beneficial laws from being passed. Perhaps the most infamous of these naked suppressions took place a few years back when Ralph Nader was making a run for President. The press would give only disparaging lip service to his candidacy, and then just as often it would misrepresent his views. The press encouraged us to believe that a vote for Ralph was a wasted vote, and that it was tantamount to a vote for the Republicans because most of Nader's supporters would have been inclined to vote Democratic.

The information controllers went so far as to prevent Nader from joining the Presidential debates in the 2000 election. Third party candidates were propagandized to be detrimental to democracy, and they were viewed as being a liability to a stable two-party system. Third party candidates are indeed injurious to our political system because they foster the presentation of new ideas, and they may not let the politicians hide behind their Coke vs. Pepsi style subterfuge, described later.

Not too surprisingly the debates referred to above were run by officials from the Republican and Democratic national committees, not by the organization that stood in as their stalking horse, the Daughters of the American Revolution *(DAR)*. That group was used to put an independent face on what was a bipartisan conspiracy. Shame on the DAR for getting its fifteen minutes of fame by allowing themselves to be manipulated this manner!

When Ralph Nader arrived at one of these debates with a valid ticket for a seat in the audience, the police refused him entry into the auditorium, and threatened him with arrest if he insisted on taking a seat. His picture, and those of the others who were also cast as *enemies,* had been placed in the so-called Book Of Faces *(persons who were to be denied admittance).*

The politicians and the interests that were behind this restriction of free assembly chose not to risk a breach in the wall of secrecy which prevents disclosure of who is truly running this country. Interfering with the controlled, two-party system might uncover that fact to the masses, they correctly reasoned. This control of process is only marginally less obnoxious than that which occurs in the banana republics that we have vehemently criticized for it.

Major corporations would like us to imagine that it is the politicians who are doing or preventing the public's bidding. But nothing could be further from the truth. A few of the real power brokers are the...
-- financial institutions
-- communications institutions
-- military industrial complex
-- automobile industries
-- health insurance industries
-- pharmaceutical industries
-- agricultural industries
-- oil, gas & coal industries
-- religious institutions

Voting for any candidate is an essentially a futile exercise. It denies the truth of corporate manipulation of this country... regardless of which party is elected.

Getting back to Nader, the Democrats to this day claim that his running for the Presidency in 2000 caused Al Gore to lose the election to George Bush, and they are still pissed at him. While I obviously am not a fan of GWB, I am less disposed to the arguments against Nader.

It is disappointing that so few people had a clue as to his justifications for running. His platform was designed to put up an offence against the pervasive influence that big business has on our legislators due to legalized bribery. While that message does not seem difficult to grasp, it did, none the less, fail to capture much of an audience. If the Democrats could not distinguish themselves enough to overcome less than one percent of the vote that was received by this third party, then perhaps they deserved to lose.

We should know by now that no matter whom the candidates may be, are our choices are always between twiddle dee dee and twiddle dee dum. Voting for candidates merely validates those who choose to corrupt themselves, this country, and deceive the voters.

One of the arguments that is perpetually put forward against voting for a third party candidate is that it represents a lost vote because that party has no chance of winning. Well what about the contention that that a *useless* vote sends a message of discontent. Hasn't the formation of the TEA party managed to influence some Republican candidates? Currently our populous is not disenchanted enough with the current state of politics to take the third-party step. This is no doubt because we have been indoctrinated since birth into believing that the current system works. Could we be more wrong? Wasn't the 2011 budget fiasco a wake-up call, even for those asleep on their couches?

The Balance of Power

The battle between the Democrats and the Republicans is not unlike the supposed competition between Pepsi and Coke for the mouths and pocketbooks of cola drinkers. This game was designed to eliminate as much outside competition as possible by ignoring or actively undermining the competing beverage companies. One could not be faulted for imagining that neither Pepsi nor Coke much cares who wins these cola wars because they are both winners as they divide up the spoils. According to press reports I have seen, they had gone so far as to prevent competing companies from buying the prized, lighted-door vending machines.

In a similar way our corporations probably don't care who appears to be in control of government because in the end it is they who are in charge with their influence peddling to both parties. They financially support both sides for a good reason. Their domination of process is very effective.

As a result of corporate influences, politicians have made the term: populist candidate virtually disappear from our lexicon. It has been relegated to the political trash heap because it is no longer a viable campaign platform for generating contributions. Years earlier the term: socialism went the same way. This was not so much because this form of economics was a dreadful idea, but because it might have reduced the corporate influence in politics. Power to the people is to be avoided at all costs.

To my way of thinking there are two ways to look at the socialism... equality and justice. In days past, the Russians practiced a form of equality where the under-educated held an inordinate amount of power, and made destructive decisions through their centralized government. The preferred form of socialism is where justice and fair play are used as guidelines for making economic decisions. In this scenario no one holds power or wealth that is disproportionate to their contribution to the whole. Excessive wealth coexisting with gross poverty would be a target of this concept... one that is regrettably ignored. And why? Can you guess who holds the power in America? A clue is that it's not the needy or under privileged.

Just like history being written by the victors, the distribution of wealth is dictated by the wealthy.

When the lack of equitable tax payments by the super rich eventually became an embarrassment to the politicians who voted in their sweetheart loopholes and benefits, a Minimum Alternate Tax was inaugurated. It was deemed that the wealthy pay some minimum tax to balance out their many benefits and tax loopholes. The result of this fix *(don't you just love that word here)* is that people with incomes in the millions of dollars can still end up paying less taxes than those with marginal incomes, such as those who work for them as domestic servants.

In 2011 the issue came up again when a billionaire stated that his tax rate was lower than that of a home employee of his. Obama took up the tax the rich fairly battle cry and was immediately met with the counter cry of class warfare by the Republican leadership. Hard as I try, the only warfare I can detect is the war by the rich who want to keep their wealth. And they offer no apology for their greed. Maybe we do need class warfare in order to correct the gross injustices that exist here and elsewhere

Insider Trading

In recent years the Securities and Exchange Commission *(SEC)* has become much more active in prosecuting insider trading on the various exchanges. But it has also had to ignore a gaping loophole in their process of jailing cheaters. Members of Congress have given themselves immunity when it comes to *(among their other unethical behaviors)* using inside information derived from conversations with corporate executives and other venues. As a result, some members have made millions of dollars from trades that would have landed you and I in jail. And as of this writing they have shown no interest in cracking down on their nefarious activities.

This is one more example of why these self-serving public servants will spend massive sums of money *(sometimes their own)* and copious hours of campaign time to secure a seat in Congress in order to enrich themselves down the road.

Then in 2012, after an exposé segment on 60 minutes, Congress did agree to abolish the practice of insider trading by Congresspersons. 99 bottles of beer on the wall - when one of them falls, 98 bottles of corruption left on the wall.

The Eric Holder Affair

In 2012 the NRA lobbied Congresspersons from both parties to hold Attorney General Eric Holder in Contempt of Congress. Their participation in this was prompted by their fear that <u>not</u> penalizing him for a failure to release documents about 'gun-walking' to smugglers would result in future legislation restricting gun sales.

After months of procrastination, diversion, and finally refusing to turn the subpoenaed documents to Congress regarding the guns given to Mexican terrorists *(the so called Fast and Furious caper)*, the House voted to issue a Contempt Of Congress citation to Attorney General Eric Holder. Holder was the first Executive Branch member to ever be sighted for criminal contempt. His refusal to provide the requested documentation was claimed to be justified owing to the support of Obama when he proclaimed Executive Privilege *(EP)* over the matter. Since Congress is not a judicial body, the citation was required to be forwarded to the Justice Department *(JD)* in Washington DC.

Well any damn fool can guess what came next. Deputy Attorney General James Cole issued a statement that the JD would not pursue the indictment of Holder based on the President's claim of EP. They went on to affirm that therefore no criminal act had been committed. The Deputy continued on by articulating that their decision follows a long-standing practice across the administrations of both parties. The only option that was left up to Congress was to issue a civil contempt citation, which does not go through the JD. Didn't happen.

Corporate Coziness

If anyone is inclined to dispute the unhealthy relationships that take place between business and government, they need look no further than the latest scandal at the Federal Aviation Agency *(FAA)* as evidence. According to the two whistleblowers who testified before Congress, the agency has routinely pressured its inspectors to ignore or soft pedal safety issues at the airlines. They testified that the FAA is cozy with airline executives and that their managers have put those personal relationships above the welfare of the flying public.

So we should ask the obvious question... don't any of these dufos have to fly on scheduled airlines? Assuming that they do, why would they be willing to put their own or their relative's lives in jeopardy for a friendship? Once again it is our genetic-emotional disposition to ignore potential problems and assume that all will take care of itself. Or in this case, it could be a darker picture of being well compensated for looking the other way.

Whistleblowers would not be needed in government or business if there were not corrupt practices going on.

We all know that our government's regulating agencies are supposed to protect us from the malpractices of industries and businesses. While this is nice in theory, it is often short on execution. One of the glaring shortcomings is the open door policy between business and government. An example of this nvolved two executives from the National Highway Traffic Safety Administration *(NHTSA)*. They joined Toyota after having been implicated in the agencies' grossly insufficient oversight of the same. Does it come as a surprise to anyone that the problems Toyota had with unintended acceleration, inability to brake, and inability to stop the engine were downplayed by the agency? Toyota was so proud of having negotiated their liability to minimal fixes that they triumphantly (*and don't you think a bit foolishly?*) posted those results in a newsletter.

It appears that the two officials mentioned above knew that they had hot chance for a lucrative position with the company that they were regulating, and they did not want to upset that applecart. One can only speculate at how often this breach of ethics takes place at government oversight agencies.

More of how business runs our government revolves around safety issues with the toxin BPA that is found in plastics used by the food industry. There have been over 100 studies from government scientists and university laboratories raising health concerns about this compound. So what was the response of the Food and Drug Administration *(FDA)*? They pronounced that these plastics are not harmful in the quantities that people would likely encounter them. Then they said in 2008 that they relied on just two research studies which were funded by the plastics industry and backed by the American Plastics Council. Council? More like a propaganda mill.

This might not be as problematical if it were not for the ignored findings of independent researchers. BPA ingestion has been linked to breast and prostate cancer, behavioral disorders, and potential reproductive problems in lab animals.

Because they had such a good example set for them, the plastic's industry is using the same model that the tobacco industry used so successfully for years…. fight the science and postpone regulation and compensation. Ultimately the science against BPA may become overwhelming, but in the mean time the sales of these plastic products go on unabated. It's all about our genetic-emotional genes because we do not know the victims.

During an exposure of government graft, it came to light in 2008 that government personnel at the Minerals Management Service *(MMS)* were enriching themselves by taking bribes from the industry that they are assigned to oversee. Not to give too much print to BP, but the infamous oil spill came about thanks in great part to the cozy factor between the regulators and regulated. BP allegedly had been permitted to violate numerous safety regulations which directly resulted in the loss of the drilling platform, eleven dead workers, and hundreds of millions of gallons of crude being spewed into the Gulf of Mexico waters.

Shortly thereafter, a senior member of the MMS retired, presumably to avoid testifying about his participation in the matter. So as it often turn out in government, white collar criminals frequently get off the hook. It's unlikely that anyone will be charged in the worker's deaths despite the overriding need to hold BP and MMS people responsible for this horrific and preventable deed.

Should we require further proof of the incest that is rampant between the government and business, one has only to look at the statistics coming out about the oil industry regulators. In 2011 it was reported that one out of five employees involved in regulating this industry had been released from some duties because they may come in contact with family members there. It appears to be a tight nit community.

Further, since mid 2008 ten people that were hired as regulators were bared for two years from working where they would come into contact with former employers. This is not rocket science to understand the logic. With the Bureau of Ocean Energy Management, 35 percent of its inspectors have been disqualified because a friend or relative works for a company that they would interact with. Prior to a recent policy change that was enacted to identify potential conflicts of interest, coziness between the regulators and regulated went on virtually unchecked.

Rampant Leniency

Government agencies that have the power to fine companies and pursue court actions have frequently turned into mister nice guy with the banking industry. How often have your heard that the defendants neither admit nor deny wrongdoing when a case is settled? This is undoubtedly the feds way of speeding up the trial process. But is it right? Is this really a punishment that would deter future infractions?

Going hand and hand with this easygoingness are the pennies on the dollar that have been accepted in court settlements. In the case of the Securities and Exchange Commission *(SEC)* v Citigroup Inc., the losses of more than $700 million to investors had a proposed settlement of just $285 thousand. To his credit, the US District judge denounced and rejected the SEC's agreement as "pocket change" when compared to the losses that were incurred. In this case Citicorp had been accused of selling slices of a Class V deal to their investors in 2007 without disclosing that they were betting against half of the assets in the deal.

In 2012 the Congress got around to passing an insider trading act specifically targeting trades that were based on the knowledge that Congresspersons picked up on the job. This was a bill that had languished for six years with virtually no support. When a TV exposé and a couple of WSJ articles brought this matter to the public's attention during Presidential campaigning, the attitude in Congress changed briefly.

The point I would demonstrate here involves the public statements that two politicians made about it. They said that this law "will help restore public trust". I guess these two deep thinkers are living in la la land, not recognizing or acknowledging the myriad of other areas where their legislative bodies' integrity is sorely lacking in integrity. That particular band-aid patch is no fix for a gaping wound.

I could go on and on, but you get the idea.

Kip's Books & Links

The books listed here are available in ebook format for Kindle™ and Nook™ readers at Amazon.com and elsewhere. Some of the shorter materials are 'ideas' booklets or excerpts from longer books. Hard copy books are available at Createspace.com. The URL links, where listed, access book previews.

Prices and page counts are subject to change.

A BETTER BATHROOM - An Ideas Guide
Construction
https://www.createspace.com/Preview/1134187

A BETTER KITCHEN - An Ideas Guide
Construction
https://www.createspace.com/Preview/1134190

AGGRESSION & BULLYING - It's Not Just Our Wiring
Human Nature

AN OUTDOOR KITCHEN - The Latest Trend?
Construction

BEFORE STARTING HOME CONSTRUCTION - What You Need To Know In Advance
Construction
https://www.createspace.com/Preview/4136208

CUSTOM HOME DOs & DON'Ts - The ULTIMATE Guide To Getting Your Custom Home DONE RIGHT!
Construction
https://www.createspace.com/Preview/1134192

DECEPTION IN AMERICA - How We Are Manipulated Big Business, Politicians, The Press & Our Indoctrinations
Government/Business/Politics
https://www.createspace.com/Preview/1134195

EVOLUTION, THE BRAIN, & RELIGION - How Evolution Made Us What We Are
Human Nature
https://www.createspace.com/Preview/1134196

EXCESSIVE EXECUTIVE COMPENSATION - What You Should Know About The Fleecing Of America By Executives & Boards
Government/Business/Politics

FOLLOWING THE CROWD - How We Fall In Line With Others
Human Nature

FREE WILL EXAMINED - The Case Against Free Will & The Case For
Determinism

FUN WITH APPETIZERS - For Those Who Like To Entertain Well
Cookbook
https://www.createspace.com/Preview/4438108

FUN WITH CARBOS - The Cookbook For Those Without A Care
Cookbook
https://www.createspace.com/Preview/4440041

FUN WITH CHICKEN - The Fowl & Seafood Cookbook That Avoids Red Meat
Cookbook
https://www.createspace.com/Preview/4441007

FUN WITH DESSERTS - The - What To Do When The
Meal Is Over - Cookbook
Cookbook
https://www.createspace.com/Preview/4444531

FUN WITH ENTREES - Getting To The Heart Of Cooking
Cookbook
https://www.createspace.com/Preview/1135491

FUN WITH FOOD – From Soup To Nuts
Cookbook
https://www.createspace.com/Preview/1143547

FUN WITH MEAT - The Carnivore's Cookbook
Cookbook
https://www.createspace.com/Preview/4436803

FUN WITH SALADS - My Take On The Classics & Others
https://www.createspace.com/Preview/1136150

FUN WITH SEAFOOD – See Food & Eat It Cookbook
Cookbook
https://www.createspace.com/Preview/4494327

FUN WITH SOUP - It's Economical, & Healthy As Well
Cookbook
https://www.createspace.com/Preview/4442511

FUN WITH WINE - Aging And Tasting Wine
An informative guide, including wine-term explanations.

HOME DESIGN GOALS - Important Considerations
Construction
https://www.createspace.com/Preview/1134209

HOME GREEN HOME - The Ins & Outs Of Home Efficiency
Construction
https://www.createspace.com/Preview/1134208

HOW BUSINESS FAILS US - What You Need To Know About Business
Corruption
Government/Business/Politics
https://www.createspace.com/Preview/1134206

HOW GOVERNMENT FAILS US - How the US government "functions" without
regard for the negative ramifications of its actions
Government/Business/Politics
https://www.createspace.com/Preview/1134204

HOW POLITICS FAILS US - What We Should Know About Our System Of
Government
Government/Business/Politics
https://www.createspace.com/Preview/1134290

HOW THE PRESS FAILS US - What They Do, And How They Contribute
Government/Business/Politics
https://www.createspace.com/Preview/1134295

HOW THE LAW FAILS US - The People That We Rely On For Our Protection
Can Be The Biggest Offenders Of It
Government/Business/Politics

HOW WE LEARN, WHY WE DON'T - Getting To Know Ourselves
https://www.createspace.com/Preview/1134212

INCONVENIENT REALITY - How Big Business Shoots Us In The Foot, & How
Congress And The Press Helped Get Us Into This Mess
https://www.createspace.com/Preview/1134213
Government/Business/Politics

INVADING YOUR PRIVACY - What You Don't Know & What You Should Know
Government/Business/Politics

MATTIAGE CAN BE FOREVER - What You Don't Know & What You Should Know
Self Help

ONE POT CLASSICS - The Comfort Food & Easy Clean-up Cookbook
Cookbook
https://www.createspace.com/Preview/1134289

POWER BREEDS ABUSE - Or To Put This Another Way... On Some Level, Power Always Leads To Corruption
Government/Business/Politics
https://www.createspace.com/Preview/1134291

SELECTING A CONTRACTOR - Making The Right Choice The First Time
Construction

SELLING & STAGING A HOME - Getting The Most From Your Efforts
Construction

SENIOR FRIENDLY HOME DESIGN - Making A House Safe
Construction

SOCIAL NETWORKING - The Downside To Exposing Yourself
Human Nature

SOLAR ENERGY EXAMINED – What You Need To Consider Before You Decide To Go Solar
Construction

THE WAR ON DRUGS - How It Harms Everyone
Government/Business/Politics

TO SELL OR REMODEL - Making The Right Decision
Construction

TRAVEL DEALS & BARGINS – Gaming The System To Win
Travel

Enjoy Reading
Kip

www.ingramcontent.com/pod-product-compliance
Lightning Source LLC
Chambersburg PA
CBHW050350290526
45785CB00006B/2706